# Stre[ss]
# for Success

## by Cathy Guisewite

Selected Cartoons from
MEN SHOULD COME WITH
INSTRUCTION BOOKLETS
Volume 1

FAWCETT CREST • NEW YORK

A Fawcett Crest Book
Published by Ballantine Books
Copyright © 1984 by Universal Press Syndicate

Cathy® is syndicated internationally by Universal Press Syndicate.

Library of Congress Catalog Card Number: 84-71442

ISBN 0-449-21017-0

This book comprises a portion of MEN SHOULD COME WITH INSTRUCTION
BOOKLETS and is reprinted by arrangement with Andrews, McMeel & Parker.

Manufactured in the United States of America

First Ballantine Books Edition: August 1986

10 9 8 7 6 5 4 3 2 1

THIS FAT AROUND MY WAIST IS FROM THE NIGHT IRVING AND I SAMPLED ALL FIVE NEW ITALIAN ICE CREAM SHOPS.

THIS FAT ON MY HIPS IS FROM THE NIGHT WE HAD SIX BOXES OF RAISINETTES AT THE MOVIES TO TIDE US OVER UNTIL DINNER.

THIS FAT ON MY FACE IS FROM THE DAY WE ATE A PIZZA WHILE WE WAITED FOR THE CHARCOAL TO HEAT UP ENOUGH TO BARBECUE A CHICKEN.

GOOD MEMORIES ARE HARD TO LOSE.

AACK! DON'T GO DOWN THAT STREET! MY HEALTH CLUB IS ON THAT STREET!
YOU CAN'T EVEN DRIVE PAST YOUR HEALTH CLUB ANY-MORE, CATHY?
...AACK! DON'T GO DOWN THAT STREET! IRVING LIVES ON THAT STREET... OOH... NOT THAT ONE, EITHER. MY BANK IS ON THAT STREET.
TO AVOID EVERYONE I WANT TO AVOID, WE HAVE TO CUT THROUGH THIS PARKING LOT, U-TURN AT THE ALLEY, WEAVE ACROSS THE BACK AND HANG A LEFT AT THE THIRD 4-WAY STOP.
THE MORE COMPLICATED MY LIFE GETS, THE CLEARER MY COURSE.

I HAD A GREAT TIME TONIGHT...
ME TOO... BUT- HO-HUM... I'M VERY TIRED.
REALLY? IT'S ONLY 11:00.
NO... I'M VERY TIRED...
WELL, OKAY... GOODNIGHT, SWEETIE.
GOOD-NIGHT...
BLINK... BLINK...
HI, CATHY. IT'S MOM. DID YOU REMEMBER TO WRAP UP THAT CHEESE FROM LUNCH?
ANSWERING MACHINE
YOU CAN COME BACK NOW, IRVING !!
Guisewite

WOMEN TODAY HAVE IT SO TOGETHER, CATHY. YOU DON'T NEED MEN ANYMORE.

HAVE IT TOGETHER?? IRVING, LOOK AT ME!

I JAMMED MY BRIEFCASE IN THE OVEN WHEN YOU CAME IN... MY BILLS ARE STUFFED IN THE SILVERWARE DRAWER... MY SKIRT IS STAPLED SHUT...

...MY HEM IS STUCK UP WITH MASKING TAPE... THREE OF MY NAILS ARE GLUED ON... AND I'M ONLY WEARING COLOGNE BECAUSE I DUG MY SWEATER OUT OF THE DIRTY CLOTHES BAG!!

THIS IS THE MOST DISGUSTING THING I'VE EVER SEEN!!!

DESTROY A MYTH, CREATE A LEGEND...